STRANGE CULTS IN AMERICA

BOB LARSON

POCKET GUIDES
Tyndale House Publishers, Inc.
Wheaton, Illinois

Adapted from *Larson's Book of Cults,* copyright 1982 by Bob Larson,
published by Tyndale House Publishers, Inc.

Scripture references are taken from the *King James Version* of the Bible,
unless otherwise indicated.

Second printing, June 1986
Library of Congress Catalog Card Number 85-52231
ISBN 0-8423-6675-X
Copyright 1986 by Bob Larson
Printed in the United States of America

CONTENTS

Why Are Cults So Attractive to Americans?

American soil has been the foremost battle-ground in the war of the cults versus Christianity.

It's ironic this struggle has occurred here. Both the devout and the deists who settled this land were committed to a transcendent faith that recognized a personal God based on the Judeo-Christian model.

> "America has a religious hunger, and it is trying to satisfy it either at quick-food drive-ins or at exotic restaurants" [William J. Petersen, *Those Curious New Cults in the 80s*].

However, the promise of free exercise of religion that originally lured people to America also has fostered utopian, communal, and apocalyptic dreams. The American vision has always been enamored with idealistic answers promising a simplistic and sacred explanation for life's purpose.

Today's cult invasion is the cultural extension of this uniquely American attitude.

CULTS IN AMERICA
—GROWING STRONGER

Its easy to develop the impression that the cults were largely a "fad" of the 1970s, a cultural phenomenon that has peaked and is now in the decline.

Not true. *The Cult Observer* (February/March 1985) reports, from a survey of fourteen cult experts, that the cults are in fact *growing* and are as strong and influential as ever.

"Several correspondents cautioned against being deceived by the decrease in media attention to cults. Betty McConahy of the Citizens Freedom Foundation explained, 'The phenomenon has become so common that it is no longer newsworthy unless "local color" or tragedy' " [*The Cult Observer*, February/March 1985].

THE APPEAL OF THE CULTS

Why are cults so attractive to many people?

In his book, *Those Curious New Cults*, author William J. Petersen suggests the following:

1. Disillusionment with American political life
2. Dehumanization by science and the computer age
3. The advent and strange appeal of the drug culture
4. Future fright—the fear of nuclear or environmental cataclysms
5. The breakdown of the family
6. Popular culture (music and literature)
7. Psychology and the occult (Jung to Joseph Rhine)
8. The decline of the church
9. The ecology crisis

For these and other reasons, an estimated 1,500 to 3,000 cult groups flourish in North American society. Their adherents range from thousands to small bands of disciples numbering a few hundred or less.

THE DEFINITION OF A CULT

What is a cult? An adequate definition evades most people. *Webster's New Collegiate Dictionary* (1984) states that a cult represents a religious body that is "unorthodox or spurious." It also cites the wider perimeter of "devotion to a great person, idea, or thing."

In Dr. Walter Martin's book *The Kingdom of the Cults,* Dr. Charles Braden is quoted as saying: "A cult . . . is any religious group which differs significantly in some one or more respects as to belief or practice from those religious groups which are regarded as the normative expression of religion in our total culture."

7

Ronald Enroth points out that the origin of the word "cult" can be traced to the Latin *cultus,* which "connotes all that is involved in worship-ritual, emotion, liturgy, and attitude."

Another way of defining cult groups is by searching for traits they have in common:

1. A *centralized authority* that tightly structures both philosophy and lifestyle.
2. A *"we" versus "they" complex,* pitting the supposedly superior insights of the cult group against a hostile outside culture.
3. A commitment for each member to *intensively proselytize* the unconverted.
4. An *entrenched isolationism* that divorces the devotee from the realities of the world at large.

THE ORIGINS OF A CULT

At their beginnings many small religious groups display sincere expressions of a humble desire to better society and follow God's will.

Soon, however, some such groups develop notions that they have special insights or revelations regarding the "truth." The founders' teachings become codified into an organized and authoritative belief system.

Then, allegiance to the founders' ideals becomes mandatory. According to Dr. Walter Martin, what develops is a "type of institutional dogmatism and a pronounced intolerance for any position but their own."

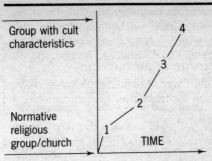

KEY
1. Small group splits from established religious body.
2. Development of special insights or revelations.
3. Revelations codified and made authoritative.
4. Allegiance made mandatory.

PROFILE OF A CULT INITIATE

Cult members, interestingly enough, are usually drawn out of established, traditional, mainstream religious groups or church denominations. To the cult member, the established church may seem sterile, unfulfilling, or ineffective in achieving social change.

Attracted to the warmth and love displayed by cult members (love-bombing), many young people become tantalized by such an affirming community with which they can identify.

Some young people are also enticed by a cult's claim to have "restored" truths that supposedly were previously lost or even undiscovered. Initiates whose religious faith is nominal and whose biblical literacy is minimal are particularly susceptible to the "new" doctrines of a cult.

Profile of an Initiate
1. Unfamiliar with biblical truth and often nominal in faith.
2. Dissatisfied with current church/established religion.
3. Attracted to the love, warmth of a cult.
4. Enticed by "new" revelation, "restored" truths.

TECHNIQUES OF A CULT

Cults generally attract prospective members with an outpouring of attention and affection called *love-bombing*. Feeling, not doctrine, is the lure. Cult leaders know that once an initiate feels a sense of meaningful belonging, he or she will more easily be mentally and doctrinally conditioned. The heart is used to trap the mind.

Love-bombing is usually accompanied by *sensory deprivation*—extreme amounts of physical activity, long periods without sleep, a diet high in carbohydrates and low in protein, severance of all family ties and former friendships—in general, inducement of fatigue and physical/mental/emotional dependence upon the cult group.

Then *intensive indoctrination* begins—a refocusing of the initiate's mind upon the cult's philosophical and theological system, with an emphasis on its ingenuity and, once again, "special revelation." At first, doctrine is presented as being normative, if not identical to the doctrinal system of the established church; the more problematic of the cult's doctrines are minimized and sometimes not even mentioned. Later, when the initiate has become more dependent on the cult, doctrinal differences are presented as being superior to the teachings of the established church.

Motivational techniques are employed to propel the initiate into action and commitment. Rewards are offered for outstanding achievement—usually in the arena of evangelizing and proselytizing. Critical thinking is discouraged. Corporate (cult) goals are emphasized.

Eventually the initiate may go through a process called *snapping*—the sudden, drastic alteration of personality. Family members, if they still have contact with the relative in the cult, may no longer recognize his or her behavior, thoughts, or beliefs.

THE MOST DANGEROUS CULTS IN AMERICA

Many "cult-watchers" rank these as among the "most dangerous" cults in America in the 1980s:

1. Unification Church
2. Scientology

3. The Way International
4. Rajneesh
5. Transcendental Meditation
6. The Children of God

In the following pages, each of these cults is examined closely. You'll find here valuable information about the cult's appeal and beliefs. In many cases, an update is provided to offer the most current news regarding the cult. A list of suggestions is offered to help you relate to members of cult groups. Finally, a list of additional resources on cults will hopefully steer you toward a deeper understanding of the cult phenomenon and its impact on America.

CHAPTER 1

The Unification Church

"The Cross is the symbol of the defeat of Christianity." This author was stunned at that statement and wondered if the speaker really meant what he said. Rev. Sun Myung Moon had harangued the audience through his Korean interpreter for more than two hours. His message was filled with many theological absurdities, but this last statement topped them all. "The Cross is the symbol of the defeat of Christianity," he repeated.

Full page newspaper ads had stirred this writer's curiosity. "Christianity in Crisis— New Hope for America," the headlines declared. The year was 1973 and few people had yet heard of this militant messiah. The word "Moonie" had not yet entered the average person's vocabulary. Today, Rev. Moon, "Lord of the Second Advent" to his disciples, has stirred international controversy.

THEOLOGY OF THE THIRD ADAM

Did he actually intend to ridicule the cross of Christ as representing the hallmark of Christianity's failures? Moon went on to explain the theology which hatched this conclusion. Before Adam had a conjugal relationship with Eve, she was sexually seduced by the serpent, none other than the Archangel Lucifer. The evil offspring of this union (Cain) became the seed from which communism sprang. Abel, Adam's child, started the lineage resulting in the spiritual democracies of South Korea and the United States. With the blood line of humanity tainted by Eve's sexual sin, God's original purpose in creating Adam and Eve was thwarted. He had wanted them to procreate a perfect human family; therefore, Christ came to Earth as a man to correct Adam's failure.

Moon says that Jesus of Nazareth was the bastard offspring of Zechariah and Mary. ("Jesus is not God himself," he states.) Since God intended for Christ spiritually and physically to redeem mankind, he needed to marry, father children, and begin rearing the perfect family. But before he could find the Eve he searched for, the Jews killed him. As a result, his death on the cross fulfilled only half of God's plan, the spiritual redemption of man. Since then, God has searched for 2,000 years to find someone who would redeem the human race by becoming the True Parent—the Third Adam, who must have a sinless life and be completely dedicated to God's will. If he qualifies, he will succeed where the First Adam (in Eden) and the Second Adam (Christ) have failed.

Such theological assertions are only a small part of the highly unorthodox worldview held by Rev. Moon. He could easily be ignored as another Oriental fanatic were it not for the fact that thousands of people worldwide receive his doctrinal fantasies as their supreme spiritual authority. As a result, this millionaire industrialist from South Korea has enslaved the minds of thousands of young people, stripped them of their personal belongings, and pressed them into virtual servitude. In doing so, he has amassed a fortune for himself and his church.

Moon Quotes

"I will conquer and subjugate the world. I am your brain."

"He [God] is living in me. I am the incarnation of himself."

"I want to have members under me who are willing to obey me even though they may have to disobey their own parents."

"In restoring a man from evil sovereignty, we must cheat."

"Master [Moon] here is more than any of those people (saints and prophets) and greater than Jesus himself."

Moon was born in 1920 as Yong Myung Moon and was reared in a Presbyterian family. His childhood clairvoyant inclinations climaxed at the age of sixteen when Moon claims he had a vision of Jesus. He claimed that Christ commissioned him to fulfill his interrupted task of physically saving humanity. Moon married his first wife in 1944 and began gathering a following. After meeting Park Moon Kim, a self-proclaimed messiah, Moon changed his name from Yong Myung Moon (Dragon Shining Moon) to Sun Myung Moon (Sun Shining Moon).

THE DIVINE PRINCIPLE

The next few years were spent in prison. Moon says he was persecuted for opposing communism, though his contemporary critics claimed that accusations of ritual sex practices were the real reason behind his incarceration. In 1954 his wife divorced him. Shortly after this he officially organized the Unification Church. Three years later he published his spiritual manifesto, *Divine Principle*. Meanwhile he searched for the perfect woman. His marriage to a fourth wife Hak Ja Han (some say he never divorced number two before going on to number three) was proclaimed as the "marriage of the Lamb" prophesied in Revelation 19. Such eccentricities brought charges of moral improprieties and excommunication from the Presbyterian church.

This rebuke certainly didn't affect his business success. His Korean conglomerates of munitions, tea, and titanium accumulated an estimated worth of $20 million. His next target for money and Moonies was the United States, where he headed in 1972.

The stage had already been set in 1959 when Young Oon Kim, an associate, brought Moon's message via an English translation of *Divine Principle*. Spiritualistic medium Arthur Ford extolled Moon as the New Age voice of religious thought.

THE AMERICAN STRATEGY

Once he arrived in America, Moon wasted no time in getting on with his job in high style. He purchased a million-dollar headquarters complex and a $625,000 residence in upstate New York. The New Yorker Hotel and Tiffany Building were also added to his real estate portfolio, with rumors of overtures to buy the Empire State Building. A large circulation newspaper called *News World* was launched and nationwide tours heralded his message. Moon defended the beleaguered Richard Nixon and was photographed with Hubert Humphrey and Ted Kennedy. His political aspirations were as exaggerated as his spiritual goals. He wanted nothing less than to organize a religious party and institute a worldwide, theocratic rule.

As Moon and his followers gained the attention of a skeptical press, a national controversy erupted. Parents charged him with brainwashing and hired deprogrammers to rescue their children from his clutches. Questions were raised regarding the legality of immigrant status for his Korean followers. Moonies swarmed Capitol Hill to cajole members of Congress. Meanwhile, other followers invaded shopping centers and airports hawking flowers and candles to the tune of millions of dollars every year.

Not so long ago, all this would have seemed like the plot line from a novel. In this case, fact is indeed stranger than fiction, providing an interesting commentary on the religious climate of America. It can't be denied that Moon's teachings obviously strike a responsive chord with many. Young people disillusioned with the institutional church and yearning for security within an authoritarian structure have been the fuel for his spiritual fuselage. Invited to a weekend retreat of flattery, smiles, and "love bombing," initiates hear nothing of Moon or his claims. It is later that the cult tactics of sensory deprivation, physical exhaustion, and intense indoctrination are used to introduce neophytes to their "True Father and Mother"—Mr. and Mrs. Moon.

LORD OF THE SECOND ADVENT
Moon's theological scheme is based on a scope of history divided into an Old Testament Age, a New Testament Age, and the present Completed Testament Age. The latter requires a new revelation of truth to supplant the Bible, and Moon's 536-page *Divine Principle* fills the bill. It was dictated, he explains, by God to him through the process of automatic handwriting. Its "truths"

were compiled only after Moon had conferred in the spirit world with Buddha, Jesus, and other notable religious figures. All bowed in acquiescence to Moon, imploring him to bring humanity the unuttered revelations supposedly mentioned by Jesus in John 16:13. Moon also reserves the option of continuing to add supernatural revelation or adjusting his "divine principle" at a future date.

Central to his belief system is the concept of a Third Adam, the Messiah and Lord of the Second Advent. Moon declares that this world savior will "appear in the East," that he will unify all religions, and that his birth date (determined by numerological calculation) was sometime about 1920. More specifically, this messiah must come from an Oriental land populated by Christians. He will be persecuted by the masses who reject him. Like John the Baptist who came as Elijah, this "Lord" will appear in a physical body.

Address/Location
The Holy Spirit Association for the Unification of World Christianity

U.S. Headquarters
1365 Connecticut Ave., N.W.
Washington, DC 20036

International Training Center
723 South Broadway
Tarrytown, NY 10591

THE KOREAN CONNECTION

Though Unification Church leaders are careful publicly to avoid naming Moon as this messiah, the deductive conclusions are inescapable. The suffering, torture, and bloodshed he claims to have endured in communist prisons is supposed to be further proof of his redemptive mission. Moon neither confirms nor denies that he is the Promised One but does purport to have personally conquered Satan. The present battle line between good and evil, God and the devil, is the 38th parallel between North and South Korea. Since the Almighty has chosen the United States as the bulwark against satanic communism, it is Moon's duty to reverse America's moral and spiritual decline.

SEX AND PURIFICATION

Moon promises more than a message. It is his duty to take up where Christ left off. The union with his present wife is presumed to result in a new humanity, not polluted by Lucifer's bloodline. Do the failed marriages of Moon disqualify him to be a messiah? "No!" Moonies respond, emphatically. His mission to save humanity is so crucial that more than one perfect woman could have been the "True Mother." God prepared several "Eves" and the first three failed. Hak Ja Han is *the* Mother of mankind who has finally been chosen of God. Sin, in Moon's estimation, is a matter of genetics, not moral choice. And salvation is a matter of being born of his physical bond or entering a marriage union chosen and blessed by him.

Knowledgeable critics charge that when the cult was small, the doctrine of "blood cleansing" (removing Lucifer's genetic interference) was accomplished by having female Unification members engage in sexual intercourse with Rev. Moon. The dramatic growth of the cult necessitated that this premise be expanded to include purification for any male who has had relations with a woman "cleansed" by Moon. Now, those who totally submit to his authority may consider their devotion to be a spiritual kind of purification not requiring sexual cohabitation.

The absolution Moon offers may require members to turn over all their financial assets to the Unification Church. Any children may be removed from personal parental guidance and placed under the church's corporate care. Prior marriages have to be ended and resolemnized by Moon. Those who are single must wait until after seven years of service to Moon before he chooses a mate for them. Some do not meet their future marriage partner until the day of the wedding, and are not allowed to consummate the

---

Text

The *Divine Principle*, by Reverend Sun Myung Moon. Moon's revelations are said to be the "things to come" referred to in John 16:13.

union until forty days thereafter. To conserve Moon's time and energy, mass wedding ceremonies are held where as many as 2,075 couples are joined in matrimony at one time.

STRANGE BELIEFS

There are many other strange beliefs held by Moon. In some cases, members are encouraged to isolate themselves from all contacts with parents and past associates. Mother and Father Moon are the True Parents (the term "Heavenly Father" is reserved for God) and the only ones worthy of devotion.

In exchange for this submission, all the necessities of life are provided. Food, clothing, and accommodations, everything from toothpaste to trousers, are served up communal-style for those members who forsake all to pound the streets selling wares to augment church income. A minimum quota is suggested (such as $100 or more a day) though some ex-members claim to have brought in as much as $1,600 in one outing. Estimated totals indicate this approach brings in about $1 million every five days.

Deliberate misrepresentation ("heavenly deceit") is used when a customer inquires regarding the destination of the proceeds. People are far more inclined to give to a "drug rehabilitation program" or to "feed starving children" than to fill the coffers of a self-anointed messiah. Members have also been known to solicit from wheelchairs in order to enhance the sympathy motives of potential contributors.

Moon's theology is a mixture of Christian concepts and spiritistic practices. He teaches that heaven is a realm of the spirit world. Hell is inconsequential because it will "pass away as heaven expands." One's destination after death depends on his spirit's "quality of life on earth; by the degree of goodness we build into them through our actions." Unlike the Christian promise of immortal perfection, Moon insists that in the afterlife his followers will experience the same "desires, dislikes, and aspirations as before death." Any spot sprinkled with soil from Korea is considered to be Holy Ground. Evil spirits may be expelled by a sprinkling of Holy Salt. An application may be surreptitiously applied from behind whenever someone considered evil enters one of their centers.

SOME OCCULT PRACTICES

Sunday mornings are set aside to pay homage to the True Parents. Rising at 5:00 A.M.,

---

Symbol
A square surrounded by a circle. Four spokes radiate from the outer circle to the center where they meet a smaller darkened sphere inside the square. The inner circle radiates spokes to the edge of the square.

---

the Church Family bows three times before a picture of Rev. and Mrs. Moon. A pledge follows in which members vow to do whatever necessary to bring about Moon's will on earth. At times, prayer sessions (with petitions directed to Moon himself) become loud, frenzied affairs. Observers report seeing some devotees sob and wail, pounding their fists on the floor in explosive outpourings of grief and exclamations of victory. Moonies were described by one reporter as jerking spasmodically "in spiritual transport like participants in a voodoo ceremony." Such traumas of self-evaluation are better than receiving a humiliating tirade from Moon. To those who fail his goals, the True Father is merciless. He scathingly attacks slothful members, accusing them of not helping to build the kingdom of heaven on earth.

From the beginning, occult practices have overshadowed Moon's approach. He admits communicating with familiar spirits by means of seances. Though the Christian ordinances of baptism and communion are avoided, the Unification Church accepts clairvoyance, automatic handwriting, and mediumistic trances. Moon confidently predicts, "As history approaches its end point, more and more people will have spiritual and psychic experiences." He promises followers that those who are completely surrendered to his precepts will witness spirit materialization of their Father (Moon). Certain members claim to have observed this phenomenon while others credit Moon with the ability to read their minds. Some initiates have been lured by dreams in which Moon and his wife have appeared to call them to service in the church. Ironically, those who consider forsaking Moon's teachings are warned that such actions may result in satanic possession.

SETBACKS

Moon has now fallen out of grace with Seoul's new governmental leaders and favorable mention of him in the press is barred in his homeland. Most Koreans seem genuinely embarrassed by Moon's image. In the United States, public consciousness of his unsavory activities is better known than the tactics of most cults.

This has created a plethora of problems. Some of his church-owned buildings in New York have been declared taxable. And the U.S. Immigration and Naturalization Service has recommended Moon's deportation based on the falsified credentials of his wife's application for permanent resident alien status. A federal grand jury in New York handed down a twelve-point indictment charging Moon and an aide with tax evasion. A court found him guilty of conspiracy to avoid taxes on $162,000 in personal income.

This unfavorable publicity forces Moon to keep his recruiting tactics at a feverish pace to balance the estimated 50 percent attrition rate of disillusioned followers. But so long as America remains a society of rootless youth, Moon's vision of hope for the future will continue to attract a sizeable following. In fact, Moon's disciples are so confident of the days ahead that church President Mose Durst now openly declares Moon to be the "second messiah" succeeding Jesus.

UPDATE
In July 1982 the Reverend Sun Myung Moon was sentenced to eighteen months at the federal prison in Danbury, Connecticut, for tax evasion.

The case drew unexpected support for Moon from a number of religious groups and churches, including the National Council of Churches and the National Association of Evangelicals, who expressed fears that Moon's conviction would open the door to government intrusion into the activities of religious groups around the country.

The Supreme Court refused to review the case in 1984, which quieted the debate, but not in time to stop sudden new public interest in the UC's theology.

In early 1985 the Unification Church mailed a public relations "package" to some 300,000 pastors and other Christian leaders across the country as an attempt to woo interest and support from established Christian churches and denominations.

Before his conviction, Moon launched *The Washington Times,* a daily newspaper competing head-to-head with *The Washington Post* in the nation's capital. The *Times* has lost more than $150 million since its inception in 1982.

Some news items have painted a portrait of the Unification Church as an organization that has a nearly unlimited source of money, that is a master at manipulating the media and other religious groups, but that has fewer followers than they actually claim.

The Washington Post (9/16/84) reported that at least $800 million has been transferred from the UC's Japan church into the American church's enterprises since 1973.

More recently, some cult experts have questioned the UC's math. Claims of 40,000 members in the U.S. church are being challenged. Some experts say that the true U.S. membership stands closer to 3,500.

The Reverend Sun Myung Moon was released from prison on August 20, 1985.

Deviations

The God depicted in *Divine Principle* is neither omnipotent nor sovereign in earth's affairs. Assigning a female nature to the Holy Spirit and ridiculing Christ's resurrection is blasphemy of the highest order. Moon's doctrine of sinless perfection by "indemnity" (forgiveness of sin by works on Moon's behalf), which can apply even to deceased ancestors, is a denial of the salvation by grace offered through Christ (Gal. 1; Eph. 2:8, 9). The warning in Matthew 24 regarding false prophets is clearly fulfilled in Moon's doctrines and claims to spiritual authority.

Scientology

Make it past the Hare Krishna chanters on the streets of any large city, and you're likely to run into a more conventionally dressed, clean-cut young man or woman offering you a "free personality analysis." Who would suspect that the 200 questions to be posed are part of the recruiting program for the Church of Scientology? Why be skeptical of "an applied religious philosophy" which offers "a clear, bright insight to help you blaze toward your mind's full potential?" After all, Dianetics (meaning "through the soul") promises to reveal "the single source of all man's insanities, psychosomatic illnesses, and neuroses."

Scientology attempts to give the appearance that it is both a science and a religion. Whatever it is, it isn't cheap. Fifty hours of Scientology counseling can cost $2,350. Some former members say they invested up to $30,000, which may explain some claims that the organization's take is over $1 million per week. With guru-like control, its founder and mentor, L. Ron Hubbard, oversees all Scientology activities from a floating fleet of ships.

Lafayette Ronald Hubbard published his book, *Dianetics—The Modern Science of Mental Health*, in 1950. It was originally intended to be his psychotherapeutic answer to the techniques of modern psychiatry. The medical community responded with alarm, forcing Hubbard to formalize his theories into a religion and thus seek tax-exempt status and freedom from governmental interference for some of his organizations. Since then, it has blossomed to command the attention of an estimated 600,000 followers and 4 million sympathizers. Hubbard's reputation as an explorer, science fiction writer, and parabotanist (he was one of the first to expound the idea of communicating with plants) has now enlarged to make him the worldwide spokesman for this fast-growing cult.

NEW SPEAK
It's difficult to understand Hubbard's teachings without a crash course in Scientology

---

Address/Location
Various world locations, including Washington, D.C., and Sussex, England

2723 West Temple St.
Los Angeles, CA 90026.

---

nomenclature. The church has found it necessary to publish a dictionary with 7,000 definitions for the use of over 3,000 Dianetic words. Ex-members claim Hubbard teaches that mankind is descended from a race of uncreated, omnipotent gods called *thetans*, who gave up their powers to enter the Material-Energy-Space-Time (MEST) world of Earth. Gradually, they evolved upward by reincarnation to become humans who could not remember their deified state. Scientologists are encouraged to awaken their dormant thetan potential by removing all mental blocks called *engrams*. By doing so they can realize their true personhood, achieving total power and control over MEST.

Engrams are said to be traumatic experiences in past lives. The "analytical mind" reasons, but the "reactive mind" simply records engrams which impede spiritual progress. Dianetics teaches the techniques for removing *(clearing)* all engrams. The one who joins Scientology, a *preclear* (PC), is said to be in need of *auditing* to discover his engrams. This is done by using a galvanometer called an E-Meter which measures the resistance to electric current by recording galvanic skin responses. As with a polygraph (lie detector), the instructor (auditor) asks a series of questions while the student holds the two tin cans of the E-Meter in his hands. (More elaborate models are available for a "donation" of $215.) Scientologists insist the auditing procedure is like a church confessional. Those who have removed the psychic hindrances of their engrams are said to be *clear.* The clear one is a thetan who has audited out his reactive mind responses.

While *Today's Health* contends that Scientology attracts the "weak, confused, lonely, and emotionally ill," there are others who genuinely look to Dianetics for altruistic reasons. Scientologists have tried to keep a clean image, publicly eschewing drugs, adultery, and premarital sex. Members are usually well-scrubbed, respectable, middle-class types. Church ministers wear the conventional black priest-suit and white collar, and even sport crosses, though they point out it isn't representative of Christ's crucifix. Scientologists talk at length about their anti-drug abuse program called Narcanon, and their efforts with prisoners and the mentally retarded.

When their teachings and tactics are questioned, Scientologists are not prone to turn the other cheek. "Ron [Hubbard] says you only get hurt when you duck," explains Jeff Dubron, a church leader. Reports have continually surfaced regarding the church's alleged tactics of harassment, intimidation, and defamation of critics. An FBI raid on church quarters revealed a hit list of

---

Symbol
A cross, believed to have ancient religious connotations, with the bar denoting matter and the vertical symbolizing spirit.

---

enemies. Included were the Mayor of Clearwater, Florida, who exposed their clandestine activities regarding a hotel purchase, and Paulette Cooper, who wrote *The Scandal of Scientology*. The government finally charged church officials with spearheading break-ins at several government offices. The purpose was to acquire documents which might embarrass and silence certain opponents. Several Scientologists, including Mary Sue Hubbard, L. Ron's wife, were found guilty of conspiring to obstruct justice.

But ethics and legality of conduct are not the foremost criteria for evaluating any system of belief. Christians are concerned with Scientology's relationship to the Bible. A major creed of L. Ron Hubbard states that "man is good." This tenet is consistent with the Dianetic belief that man is descended from the gods and may someday evolve to reclaim his thetan potential. Other doctrines and practices include astral travel, regression to past lives, and the "urge toward existence as spirits" (Scientology Dynamic number seven).

Hubbard sails the seas with his Sea Org (organization) claiming that his teachings are "the road to spiritual freedom." Those who question the compatability of Scientology and Christianity need to be reminded that Hubbard declares Dianetics to be "the spiritual heir of Buddhism in the Western world." The regal thirty-room mansion and fifty-seven acre estate the church occupies in England symbolize Scientology's success on Earth. But Christians who are preparing for life after death feel a sense of compassionate concern for those who fruitlessly search for meaning in nonexistent past lives.

UPDATE
Decisions in 1984 by two judges, one in the United States and one in Great Britain, condemned the Church of Scientology as "sinister" and "dangerous," citing evidence of the church's involvement in illegal and unethical practices.

The London high court judge was ruling in a child custody case. The California judge was ruling in a Scientology suit against former member Gerald Armstrong to recover, and keep out of evidence, copies of documents that he had made in connection with a church-approved biography of Scientology founder L. Ron Hubbard.

The U.S. Tax Court in Washington, D.C., ruled in late 1984 that the Church of Scien-

---

Deviations
Occult practices of age regression and astral travel are based on theories of reincarnation. Extrabiblical information regarding man's origin (as a god called *thetan*) and mystical beliefs regarding the relationship of spirit and matter are essential to Dianetics. Man is good, Christ was merely a "cleared" individual, and the existence of an eternal heaven and hell is denied.

tology of California does not qualify as a tax exempt religious organization because of its substantial commercial operations, some of which have earned it a "handsome profit." Courts in Germany also designated the church a "business organization," refusing it nonprofit status.

In April of 1985, a libel suit filed in Los Angeles by the church was dismissed because founder L. Ron Hubbard failed to appear for a deposition ordered in the case. Hubbard has not been seen in public since 1980.

Despite claims by church officials of increases in membership, former Scientology executives believe bitter internal battles between young insurgents and the "old timers" they seek to replace have caused massive defections. Meanwhile, various lawsuits (one of which resulted in a decision against the church and L. Ron Hubbard to the tune of $39 million for "wanton misconduct" against a Portland, Oregon, woman; it has since been declared a mistrial), indictments, and government investigations (Canada is currently investigating the church on charges of theft, possession of property and documents obtained by criminal means, and breach of trust), continue to exert pressure on the Scientology organization and leaders.

CHAPTER 3

The Way International

What happened when four clean-cut young people (two male, two female) descended upon a small, midwestern town and took up residence, calling themselves "dedicated servants of God"? Plenty. Local citizens were alarmed when they found out that the new visitors were luring young people into The Way. The faithful four held a public meeting and acknowledged that the $200 "voluntary" fee required for their Power for Abundant Living course was, in fact, mandatory. No one is admitted without prepayment of the "donation."

The majority of people in this sedate community felt their provincial charm had excluded them from the cult incursion found in big cities. But this invasion of The Way Corporation sent local citizens scampering for information as to whether or not The Way is really *the* way of Jesus Christ. Here's what they found out.

In 1957 a United Church of Christ minister, Victor Paul Wierwille, resigned his Van Wert, Ohio, pulpit to set up his own independent ministry. Wierwille began informing his followers that in 1942 God had spoken to him audibly. The message was simple: "God told me he would teach me the Word as it has not been known since the first century, if I would teach it to others." Sometimes the message is carried by rock bands like Takit and the Take a Stand Caravan which presents both music and drama. No one can question Wierwille's success. Membership in The Way is estimated between 40,000 to 100,000 in sixty-two countries.

New believers are enticed and inducted by Wierwille's Power for Abundant Living (PFAL) Sessions. Over a period of thirty-six hours, the initiates listen to tape or video recordings of Wierwille's teachings. No notes are allowed and only ten minute breaks are permitted every three hours. Questions are not permitted during the three-week course, which is strong on indoctrination but weak on objective inquiry.

PFAL sessions center on Wierwille's teaching that about 85 percent of what is believed as being Christian is not Christian if the Bible is right. Wierwille's system of theology blends elements of Armstrongism and Jehovah's Witnesses' beliefs with a mixture of orthodox doctrines. His book, *Jesus Christ Is Not God,* explains his position that "Jesus Christ is not God but the Son of God. . . . If Jesus Christ is God, we have not yet been redeemed. . . . Jesus Christ was not literally with God in the beginning; neither does he have all the assets of God."

The Way not only denies the Trinity and Christ's divinity and incarnation, but also teaches that Christ was resurrected on Saturday, and that four (not two) were crucified next to Jesus. Only believers after Pentecost will be saved, and they must remain dead until the final resurrection. Water baptism is discouraged in favor of holy spirit (lower-cased "h" and "s") baptism accompanied by speaking in tongues, a technique which, unlike its spontaneous charismatic counterpart, is "taught." Members are encouraged to cultivate this glossolalia thirty minutes every morning because it is an indispensable part of salvation.

LICENSE TO SIN?

Opponents and some ex-members claim that far worse heretical goings-on take place. They argue that Wierwille's extreme Calvinism has led to sexual indulgences based on the theory that once you're saved, sinful practices are no longer forbidden. Some have even charged that extreme licentiousness is

---

Address/Location

The Way International
Box 328
New Knoxville, OH 45871

The Way College
1300 West 12th Avenue
Emporia, KS 66801

---

found among the advanced groups in The Way International. Such conduct is said to be based on Wierwille's teaching that once one is saved he can no longer sin "in his spirit," although he can still sin in his body. This is construed by certain of his followers to be permission for smoking, drinking, drug taking, and even fornication. Other eyebrows were raised when a quadriplegic sued Wierwille for $300,000, claiming that he had given The Way $210,000 with the promise he'd be healed in a year's time. (The Way teaches a 15 percent tithe called "abundant sharing.") Some skeptics also point with alarm to the armed, private police force that watches over the 147-acre world headquarters of the cult near New Knoxville, Ohio. Rumors persist that some members hold marksmanship classes at the organization's Bible College in Emporia, Kansas, and on their 105-acre ranch near Gunnison, Colorado. Way officials say the courses are for hunting safety. Former members charge that it's all part of a plan "to take to the streets and defend the Word."

Such charges contrast with The Way terminology which includes evangelical phrases such as "born again," "Jesus Christ our Savior," and "the Word of God is the Will of God." The Way, like many cults, deceives many young Christians by using semantic deceptions which allow it to define words according to its own perception. When young "WOW Ambassadors" ("Word Over the World") are confronted with these semantic inconsistencies, they conveniently respond, "You'll have to write or call our headquarters about that."

Wierwille claims his organization is not a church but rather a "biblical research teaching and fellowship ministry." Such fellowships are called twigs (each individual member is called a leaf). Twigs are grouped into branches, and several branches make a limb. Limbs are then organized into trunks, with all trunks leading to the root at New Knoxville, Ohio.

Youthful followers of The Way are exuberant and even arrogant at times when ridiculing orthodox beliefs. They mock the "martyr, self-sacrifice" attitude of traditional Christians. "God dying on a cross is a standard by which man can achieve his own righteous-

---

Deviations

Wierwille's interpretation of the Bible is considered to be *the* Word. No attempt is made to remain faithful to the objectively tested text of the Bible. He rejects the doctrine of the Holy Trinity, seeing God as one Person (the Father) who is holy and spirit and therefore can be called "the Holy Spirit." This Holy Spirit is to be distinguished from "holy spirit" which is God's gift of spirit-life to those who turn to him in repentance. Wierwille denies the absolute deity of the Lord Jesus Christ, using sophisticated Unitarian arguments to say that Jesus Christ is not eternal and was created by God the Father.

ness. It is an image that binds man into continuous slavery and self-idolatry," wrote one student in the official newspaper of The Way College of Emporia. Such language, along with their strange nomenclature of "Bless Patrol," "First Family Corps," and "Limb Leader," leaves the average evangelical a little bewildered. Though many of Wierwille's followers are sincere, their belligerence may stem from a disillusioned background in orthodox but sterile churches. The evangelical's best response is not one of strident counterattacks, but a compassioned example of Christian faith which will cause the disciples of Wierwille to question if The Way really is *the* Way of John 14:6.

UPDATE

The Reverend Victor Paul Wierwille, founder of The Way International, died in May of 1985 at the age of 68. Three trustees, Donald Wierwille, Howard Allen, and Craig Martindale (the president of The Way since 1982) now legally control all The Way's operations and assets.

The Way is currently estimated to have a membership of 100,000 to 120,000, with Power for Abundant Living graduates in 77 countries, and active ministries in 44 of the 163 nations of the world. Some of the properties of The Way include 80 acres in New Mexico, 124 acres in Indiana, 124 acres in Scotland, and training locations in Chile, Venezuela, and Argentina. Scotland also became the site of The Way's first European College of Biblical Research in early 1985.

The group reported an income of $27.1 million for the fiscal year ending September 1984, with expenses of $22.7 million and $4.4 million for the expansion of its work. The following year, the Internal Revenue Service revoked The Way's tax-exempt status.

The United Families Association was formed in 1981 to combat negative publicity. Only Power for Abundant Living graduates may join the association.

In early June of 1984 fifty-two couples were married in a mass ceremony at The Way's biblical college in Kansas. The "Victor Paul Wierwille Word Over the World Auditorium," which cost more than $5 million to construct, was dedicated in March of 1985.

Symbols
Slogans such as "One God," and "The Word means what it says and says what it means."

Text
John 14:6, though Wierwille denies the substitutionary atonement of Christ and the propitiatory blood sacrifice of the cross.

Rajneesh

To most mystical gurus, sex, drugs, and hedonism are impediments on the path to enlightenment. Not to Bhagwan Shree Rajneesh. "I don't profess anything," he declares, and his disciples act accordingly. For students of Eastern religions who consider asceticism too confining, this is it. Until recently, all one had to do was grab the next plane to Poona, India (a route taken by notables such as Diana Ross, Ruth Carter Stapleton, and 50,000 others).

Once there, all clothes were shed for the orange robes one sees everywhere. Candidates for Rajneesh's brand of spirituality must prostrate themselves the moment Rajneesh enters the room. The seeker then receives a new Hindi name and a beaded necklace with Rajneesh's face in a locket. One important warning: devotees must wash thoroughly—especially their hair. Though he lays claim to being a "living God beyond time in a state of continuous bliss," Rajneesh has diabetes and a horrible case of asthma. Guards stand ready to sniff the hair of each entrant whose every lock must be clean and free from oil before being allowed into his "divine" presence.

Bhagwan's teachings abound in eighty books and more than 500 tapes. The message is simple—anything goes. He preaches indiscriminate premarital sex, open marriages, and the abolition of the family, which he says is "the biggest threat to human progress." In his perception of religion, Christianity is a "cult," and even the Pope and Mother Teresa receive his castigation. Traditional *sanyasis* (holy men who meditate and renounce the world) may pursue the path to God for years. The Poona guru offers the state of *sanyas,* with all of its bliss, immediately. *"Neosanyas,"* he calls it. "Westerners want things quickly, so we give it to them right away." He promises nothing less than "freedom from everything!"

For years, the balded and bearded Rajneesh was referred to as India's sex-guru.

Address/Location
Primary U.S. Rajneesh Meditation Centers:

Chidvilas
154 Valley Road
Montclair, NJ 07042

Geetam Rajneesh Sanyas Ashram
Box 576 E
Lucerne, CA 92356

Antelope, OR

At his resort in Rajasthan State he dispensed *tantric* (sex) yoga and meditation. Western pilgrims at his Poona *ashram* received more of the same. Adhering to this admonition that "the path to desirelessness is through desire," they would smoke pot, disrobe, dance, jump up and down, and pursue sex however and with whomever they wished. The sterilization of female members avoids having to cope with one possible consequence of such libertine ways.

Such antics have attracted 200,000 followers in 500 centers worldwide (100 of them in the U.S.). The estimated income totals between $5 million to $7 million a year, with Rajneesh being chauffeured about in a Rolls Royce Silver Shadow.

Born nearly a half century ago as Rajneesh Chandra Mohan, Bhagwan Shree Rajneesh ("The Blessed One Who Has Recognized Himself As God") was raised as a Jain in a small village in Madhya Pradesh province. After receiving a master's degree in philosophy, he served for a while as a professor. In 1966 he left the teaching profession to fulfill what he saw as God's plan for his life—spiritually transforming humanity. Various techniques are suggested as to how one may achieve this goal on an individual level.

REBIRTHING

Meditation at Bhagwan's *ashram* goes through five stages, from hyperventilative breathing to Sufi dancing. Participants are often required to wear blindfolds, and many discard their clothing. Since Rajneesh sees the logical mind as a barrier to spiritual progress, it is stilled by such exercises as staring at his picture without blinking for an hour. Even his endless list of irrelevant rules is designed to rid one's thinking of questioning processes. He also encourages "rebirthing," a state of returning mentally and emotionally to mother's womb before the traumas of birth. Eventually, disciples may believe they are actually rebirthing to previous incarnations; the idea is to rid the subconscious of any neuroses. Ultimate illumination comes when Bhagwan presses his thumb into the center of the initiate's forehead to awaken the mystical third eye.

The Poona *ashram* usually had approximately 5,000 to 7,000 in residence at any given time. As Rajneesh attempted to create a communal theocratic state, area citizens were offended by the way his followers displayed uninhibited sexual affections in public. Circulated stories about erotic licentiousness and physical violence inside the *ashram* walls eventually provoked harassment from the townspeople. To escape the criticism

---

Text
Hindu scriptures and Rajneesh's books, including *Beyond and Beyond* and *Above All, Don't Wobble*.

(and avoid a crackdown from Indian tax officials), Rajneesh packed up his collector's 150,000-volume library and headed for New York, along with twelve tons of luggage.

FROM INDIA TO OREGON
For years, he had been seeking "a new site, isolated from the outside world." As the dismantling of the Poona *ashram* was taking place, word surfaced that officials of the Chidvilas Rajneesh Meditation Center had already purchased (with $1.5 million in cash) more than 100 square miles of ranch land near Antelope, Oregon (120 miles southeast of Portland). Disciples attending his meditation sessions would observe the sex-guru sitting motionless for long periods of time as he entered a self-proclaimed period of "speaking through silence." It is now apparent that Rajneesh was formulating plans to establish the world's largest spiritual community on these shores—much to the chagrin of many solid Oregonians!

UPDATE
The population of the city of Rajneeshpuram, Oregon, consists mostly of affluent, white, married professionals in their early thirties, many with advanced academic degrees. However, when a Portland-based research company was commissioned by the Rajneesh to poll the city's seven surrounding counties, they reported finding unprecedented at-

titudes of suspicion, anger, and fear toward Rajneesh's followers.

Rajneeshpuram school officials filed suit to force an Oregon School Superintendent to restore $18,000 per month in state aid. He had cut off the aid on grounds that it benefited a religious organization, thereby violating constitutional guarantees of separation of church and state.

In January of 1985, Oregon imposed a total of $1.4 million in fines on the Rajneesh Investment Corporation and the Rajneesh Neo-Sanyas International Commune for violations of the state electrical code in the construction of buildings in Rajneeshpuram.

Oregon voter registration laws may be changed as a result of the attempt last fall by followers of Rajneesh to register several thousand street people they had bused in from all over the country. Seven of the New York-based Guardian Angels were arrested while protesting alleged mistreatment of these street people, who were "dumped" after deciding not to stay at the commune.

Deviations

Bhagwan Shree Rajneesh departs from traditional Hindu morality as well as biblical standards of sexuality. Man is the center of determining what conduct is permissible. While Christianity enhances self-identity, Rajneesh seems to destroy one's emotionally protective barriers of self-worth.

The Angels had chained themselves to the door of a Rajneesh-owned hotel.

Oregon courts may invalidate Rajneeshpuram's incorporation as a legal city and enforce the arrest of some of the residents for violating immigration law. Leaders of the commune have threatened violence should the state try to do this.

The Rajneesh Foundation Europe was launched in November 1984 with a 50,000-Swiss-franc account in a Zurich bank. The Foundation's statutes declare it to be a nonprofit organization for furthering the Rajneesh's religious teachings.

While just three years ago the Rajneeshees claimed to have 575 meditation centers operating in thirty-two countries, a book published by the International Foundation listed only nineteen centers in ten countries. Membership and operations at home and abroad have shrunk dramatically in the last three years.

In the fall of 1985, defections of key leaders and counter-charges of spying and attempted murder created international press attention. Rajneesh claimed that during his three years of silence, Ma Anand Sheela (his trusted secretary) had misrepresented his teachings. Sheela responded by calling Rajneesh "corrupt," saying he sells "blue skies called enlightenment" while craving more Rolls Royces (Rajneesh owned more than ninety).

Transcendental Meditation

He can't trademark the name. The words "transcendental" and "meditation" are not exclusively definitive. And even the Maharishi Mahesh Yogi acknowledges in his writings that some Hindus believe this ancient spiritual discipline was conveyed to man centuries ago by one of their gods, Lord Krishna.

Worse yet for the Maharishi (devout disciples insist "the" must be dropped when referring to him), the pretense that TM (as it is popularly known) "isn't a religion" is no longer defensible. On October 19, 1977, U. S. District Judge H. Curtis Meanor issued an extensive eighty-two-page opinion upholding the plaintiff's claim regarding the religious nature of Transcendental Meditation. In Judge Meanor's words, "No inference was possible except that the teachings of SCI/TM and the *puja* are religious in nature. No other inference is 'permissible' or reasonable, especially because the court is dealing with the meaning of the constitutional term and not with a factual dispute. . . ." Seventeen months later, the United States Court of Appeals for the Third Circuit, sitting in Philadelphia, affirmed this ruling.

The legal opinion regarding TM is of value to those Christians concerned about its incursions into public schools, prisons, the military, and other government-funded institutions. Government grants (seventeen in all at one time, including $21,540 from the Department of Health, Education and Welfare destined to show 150 high school faculty members how to teach TM) may grind to a halt. But with an estimated one million adherents in the United States alone, TM isn't going to fade away quickly. Senators, sports stars, movie idols, businessmen, and even doctors continue to tout its benefits. And Americans who are generally ignorant of religious traditions outside of the Judeo-Christian model may dismiss references to Hindu gods as so much gobbledygook. The old Yankee maxim, "If it works . . ." could yet give impetus to the Maharishi's plans for the future.

WELCOME TO L.A.
Maharishi Mahesh Yogi was born Mahesh Brasad Warma, 1911, in Jabalpur, Madhya Pradesh, India. At thirty-one years of age he graduated from Allahabad University with a degree in physics. He worked for a while in a factory until crossing paths with Swami Brahmananda Saraswati, Jagadguru, Bhag-

wan Shankaracharya of Jyotir Math (commonly known as Guru Dev—"Divine Teacher"). Guru Dev had left his home at age nine to seek enlightenment. Under the teachings of Swami Krishanand Saraswati, Guru Dev achieved his god-realization and became known as an *avatar,* a manifestation of the divine.

Guru Dev had revived a technique of meditation which originated from the Hindu monastic tradition of Shankara, a philosopher who established the practice in the ninth century A.D. For twelve years, Maharishi ("Great Sage"—a name he adopted in 1956) was the favorite student of Guru Dev. When his spiritual mentor died in 1953, Maharishi retreated to a Himalayan cave for two years. In 1958 he ended up in Madras where during a lecture he spontaneously announced a plan to spread TM all over the world. He formed the International Meditation Society and headed for the West. In Los Angeles, he chartered the Spiritual Regeneration Movement in 1959. Nothing much else happened until 1967.

Flower-power was in bloom, but the sex- and drug-crazed ways of the Beatles had brought the Fab Four disillusionment and frustration. George Harrison met the Maharishi and persuaded Ringo, Paul, and

Address/Location

TM centers in 140 countries and approximately 400 U.S. cities.

John to join him on a pilgrimage to India. There the Beatles, with Mia Farrow in tow, sat at the Maharishi's feet to be schooled in the ancient Vedic practice of transcendental meditation. The Rolling Stones and the Beach Boys joined the bandwagon. Of the latter group, Mike Love and Al Jardine became TM teachers. Brian Wilson augmented the faith of his comrades by lyrically declaring, "Transcendental Meditation, it works real good/More, much more than I thought it would." With such heady endorsements, the Maharishi confidently boasted, "I shall bring fulfillment to the hippie movement."

The promises were euphoric. Maharishi confidently predicted that just 1 percent of the population practicing TM in any locality would reduce crime and empty the hospitals. Many victims of stress and hypertension gave glowing testimonials. Some argued that such relief was merely due to an anticipatory attitude aided by the forty minutes of restful posture which TM required each day. But supporters seemed to far outnumber detractors until the bubble of optimism burst.

"We were wrong," the Beatles concluded, with John accusing the Maharishi of being a "lecherous womanizer." His following was nearly defunct and crowds no longer seemed charmed by his Hinduistic platitudes. Though he had once hobnobbed with celebrity luminaries, the Maharishi headed home with the pronouncement, "I know that I have failed. My mission is over."

Then he decided to revamp his entire approach and vocabulary. His resplendent beard and hypnotically dark eyes disappeared from American TV screens. But not for long.

BACK TO THE DRAWING BOARD

Religious terminology was dropped in favor of psychological and scientific language. The Spiritual Regeneration Movement became the Science of Creative Intelligence, and the Maharishi presented an image of a friendly psychotherapist rather than a Hindu monk. His inner circle may have heard him call the *Bhagavad-Gita* "an anchor for the ship of life sailing on the turbulent waves of time." But outsiders only heard the oft-repeated litany, "It's not a religion."

The ruse worked. By the mid-seventies, more than one million Americans had tried TM. Seven thousand teachers were propagating the Maharishi's gospel in more than 100 U.S. centers. Income jumped to over $20 million a year as 30,000-40,000 followers a month joined the movement to meditation. For an introductory fee of $55 for college students and $125 for adults (now up to $85 and $165), anyone was guaranteed inner peace. Best of all, there was no renunciation of materialism nor desire in the Buddhist

---

Text
Hindu Vedic scriptures, including the *Bhagavad-Gita,* which the Maharishi views as an "indispensable" religious document.

tradition, and no repentance of sin nor reformation of character in the Christian tradition.

Though TM has popularized the terms "meditation" and "mantra," most people are still a little vague about their precise definitions. They mean more than "deep thinking" and "a funny sounding word." To understand their usage in TM, it is necessary to decipher the religious framework of the Maharishi's entire system.

The religious philosophy of the Maharishi is rooted in Vedantic Hinduism. God is a pantheistic, pervasive Absolute Being *(Brahman)*. Even man's inner self is part of this divine Being. In Christianity, man's dilemma is separation by sin from a transcendent deity. The Maharishi sees man's foremost problem as alienation from his true Being. Salvation is derived by contacting this inner state of pure-consciousness. Meditation is the key to transcending ("going beyond") the three levels of normal consciousness to the fourth state where one is cognizant of his soul's true nature.

Three additional levels exist: cosmic consciousness, complete God consciousness, and Unity consciousness. Beginners in TM hear only about the first four, but the Maharishi's ultimate goal is to eventually lead all humanity to Unity consciousness. At that point, the meditator is liberated from the karmic cycles of reincarnation by achieving sinlessness.

For the present, the Maharishi is content with introducing adherents to the fourth level of consciousness. But what the meditator may not realize is that the interpretation of the process is based on assumptions which represent a systematic approach to Hindu theology. At the heart of this hypothesis is the mantra. Representatives of the Maharishi insist it is only a vibratory sound with "no denotive meaning." To the contrary, Hindu tradition believes that such words or syllables have supernatural powers, often invoking a deity who is believed to embody the sound.

TM as prescribed by the Maharishi requires the initiate to sit with eyes closed in a quiet, relaxed position, twenty minutes in the morning and again in the evening. All the while his mind repeats the Sanskrit word deemed to be his own personal mantra. This mantra is the means of "diving" to the depths of the mind's ocean, delving into ever subtler recesses of thought. No mental discipline is necessary. The mantra does it all. Just let the mind go out of gear and coast to its desired destiny of fulfillment.

In the process, one's deepest thoughts emerge and dissipate like tiny champagne bubbles. As the incantation progresses, the meditator is supposed to be relieving tension and disposing of stress. When the source of

---

Symbol
The letters T and M, capitalized and appearing together (TM) as an abbreviated reference to Transcendental Meditation.

all thought is reached, the chanter has available "a reservoir of energy, intelligence, and happiness." Only 73,500 minutes of meditation later, the faithful have hope of absolute union with Being, provided they never meditate before bed nor after a meal.

Mantras aren't easy to acquire. The introductory fee is a mandatory requirement. Every meditator must also undergo an initiation ceremony which is distinctly idolatrous in nature. The initiate, with fruit, flowers, and a white handerchief in hand, takes off his shoes and enters a candle-lit room. Then, the instructor directs the initiate to lay these items on a flower-banked altar which features a color portrait of Guru Dev. Incense pervades the atmosphere. Finally, the teacher kneels before the altar and begins to sing in Sanskrit. The initiate may stand or kneel, too, as he listens to this ten-minute recitation.

When TM first became popular, most people didn't question this part of the ceremony. They were told it was "not a religious observance" but merely an opportunity for the teacher to "express his gratitude to the tradition from which TM comes." Apprehensive students were said to be "witnessing" the ritual, "not participating." Christian researchers weren't placated by this innocuous tale, and persisted in their attempts to uncover the truth about the proceedings. What they discovered came as no shock.

The TM initiation song is actually a devotional Hindu hymn called a *puja*. Guru Dev's picture represents a *murti,* the literal embodiment of God in corporeal form. While singing the *puja* (which means "worship") the instructor first invokes the favor and presence of the Hindu gods. Then he presents seventeen offerings to Guru Dev before finally praising him (personified by his picture-idol) as an incarnation of deity.

After this incantation, the teacher leans toward the initiate and whispers a mantra in his ear. The secret word is supposed to be his very own specialized mantra, chosen for him by a Maharishi-trained instructor. The mantra must never be divulged to an outsider, even a spouse, or it will lose its magical powers. The meditator's own particular temperament, personality, and profession have presumably been analyzed to determine *the* mantra which will produce the appropriate psychic vibrations. In fact, recent investigation has shown that only sixteen TM mantras actually exist, and these are dispensed according to age.

Does the mantra really work? Though the Maharishi's organizations publish volumes of information about research studies, most non-TM scientists are skeptical. No body of findings exists that has been subject to the proper, objective controls which would substantiate the claims of TM. The American Association for the Advancement of Science evaluated TM as to its stress-reducing capabilities. Tests concluded that the Maharishi's meditation techniques "produced no measureable change whatever in the body's basic metabolism, and further, TM did not induce a unique state of consciousness."

DANGEROUS CONSEQUENCES

Evangelical critics charge that in the absence of provable positive effects, there are dangerous spiritual consequences. To begin with, TM conditions the meditator's view of reality and religion, predisposing him toward an Eastern concept of man and God. The guilt of sin can be neutralized by inducing a false sense of serenity replacing the stress caused by conviction. Demonic phenomena may result because spiritual defense mechanisms become ineffective when the mind enters a state of passivity. Some meditators report a "black-out phenomenon," waking up hours after starting to chant, unable to remember what has happened. In addition, some advanced meditators exhibit neuroses and psychoses resulting from the practice of "unstressing," the procedure of shedding karma from one's present and past lives through prolonged meditation.

To counter such criticism and to legitimize his efforts, the Maharishi has tried to further refurbish his image. God-name mantras have been dropped and the organizational entity has been subdivided. The TM empire now includes: World Plan Executive Council, Student International Meditation Society, American Foundation for Creative Intelligence, American Meditation Society, Maharishi International University (in Fairfield, Iowa), Maharishi European Research University, Institute for Fitness and Athletic Excellence, and Affiliated Organizational Conglomerate. The Maharishi directs the activities of all these organs from his international headquarters in the Swiss village of Seelisberg.

As the number of new converts plunged to an estimated low of 4,000 per month in the late seventies, TM launched its most controversial aspect—the *Sidhi* program. *(Siddhi* is a Sanskrit term denoting supernatural, occult powers. The Maharishi has adopted the variant spelling *Sidhi* for trademark purposes.) A *Sidha* (one who has completed Sidhi training) spends from

---

Deviations

The TM initiation ceremony violates the First Commandment. Matthew 6:7 denounces the chanting of mantras. Maharishi Mahesh Yogi's monist view of the universe is not compatible with the scriptural presentation of a personal God, who as Creator, is distinct from his creation. Christian meditation is an outward concentration on the Word and ways of God, whereas TM is a passive, selfish, inward withdrawal from reality. The repetitious sensory stimulation dulls the conscious mind, and makes it vulnerable to evil invasion. Christ's blood atonement is rejected in the Maharishi's statement, "[TM] is the only way to salvation and success in life."

$3,000 to $5,000 to reach an enlightened state of infinite compassion. He is also supposed to have the ability to walk through walls, become invisible, and levitate.

Advanced meditators claim to have mastered dematerialization and flying, "just like Peter Pan." In mattress-filled rooms ("landings are unusually bumpy"), the Maharishi's most ardent followers say they begin by hopping, then floating, in preparation for flight. Leaders claim that nearly 4,000 have conquered the art, but offers by the press of up to $10,000 to witness a meditator on the wing have gone unclaimed. The validity of the Sidhi program is undercut by the Maharishi's preferred form of transportation—two Rolls Royces and his private helicopter which await him outside his residence.

Whether TM's vaunted relief from tension will enhance the moral virtue claimed by this pronouncement is yet to be proven. The mantras may give meditators an improved sense of well-being. But it remains to be seen whether such positive feelings will also produce individuals who act in accordance with sound ethics.

UPDATE
In April 1985, Transcendental Meditation began construction of a large international spiritual center and residential-work complex in Lelystad, Holland. The $10 million project will include a restaurant, meditation

hall, schools, computer software factories, and offices.

In September 1984, an affiliate of the Maharishi in the Philippines bought controlling interest in the privately run University of the East, the Philippines' largest university with an enrollment of 47,000 students. When it was discovered that the Maharishi was seeking to gain dominance in Centro Escolar University, concern over the group's activities heightened. Education Minister Jaime Laya finally canceled the operating permit for U.E., after 20,000 protesters, mostly students and teachers from U.E. and C.E.U., demonstrated in front of the ministry offices. They condemned the Maharishi's "foreign intrusion."

The Maharishi organized an estimated 3,000 to 5,000 of his followers for a special gathering at Maharishi International University in December of 1983. The stated purpose was to create a harmonious effect that would neutralize negative influences in the world.

Technology of the Unified Field is Maharishi's latest project. It combines TM with the advanced *Sidhi* program.

CHAPTER
6

Children of God

"They went out from us, but they were not of us." The Apostle John's appraisal of first century heretics (1 John 2:19) might well describe how early Jesus Movement pioneers feel about the Children of God. (In 1978 the name Children of God was changed to Family of Love to avoid identification with the bad publicity attached to the COG image.)

The far-flung clan of David "Moses" Berg had once spanned seventy-two countries with an estimated membership nearing 10,000. Today, less than 1,000 hard-core followers may remain. Berg's "Royal Family" empire is in shambles, with children, in-laws, and even his legal wife having deserted him.

David Berg was the son of a devout Christian and Missionary Alliance couple. His father, Hjalmer, pastored and taught at a Christian college. Virginia, his mother, was a radio evangelist. David married Jane Berg in 1944 and entered Christian service as an evangelist. Berg gradually soured on organized religion and was associated with fringe religionist O. L. Jaguers and TV evangelist Fred Jordan. During the earlier years of the West Coast Jesus Revolution, Berg joined his mother in directing a Teen Challenge coffeehouse. It was there that his radicalized, antiestablishment gospel took root among religiously zealous hippies.

In 1969 Berg left the coffeehouse and with about fifty followers headed on a trek to Arizona, later described as a time analogous to Israel's wanderings in the wilderness. The rag-tag group took organized form with members assuming new biblical names. Twelve groups were formed, named and patterned after Israel's twelve tribes. They couldn't go back to California because Berg had twice "prophesied" the exact date the entire wicked state would slide into the ocean. Their meandering ended when Fred Jordan invited them to locate on his Texas Soul Clinic Missionary Ranch.

Maria, a Tucson church secretary, joined the movement and later was elevated to the status of Berg's mistress. (Jane was nicknamed "Mother Eve" and was allowed certain sleeping "rights" with David. In 1980 she ran off with another COG member.)

Text
The Bible, but more prominently the periodic MO letters, rambling discourses by which Berg communicates with his followers.

THE MO LETTERS

When the first wave of controversy hit the COG with charges of kidnapping and brainwashing, Jordan kicked the cult out. By this time, the COG numbered at least 2,000 and had the strength to go it alone. Communal organizations were divided into colonies, and a subsidiary called THANK COG (consisting of favorably disposed parents of COG members) was activated to counter the charges of FREE COG parents who claimed their offspring were unfairly controlled by Berg. To communicate with his increasingly fragmented followers, Berg hit upon the concept of circulating periodic newsletters that came to be called "MO Letters."

The rambling and grammatically shabby content of Berg's epistles evolved into what were considered divinely commissioned pronouncements. MO letters were said to be God's inspired Word for today, far superior to what was written in the Bible thousands of years ago. Letters were categorized according to the ranks of insiders who had access to them. Considering the pornographic overtones of Berg's sexual preoccupation, it was understandably wise of him to restrict certain MO letters to his immediate intimates.

Though no official systematic theology was promulgated, a philosophical and methodological structure did emerge. A pyramidal system of leadership (with Berg at the apex) placed "babes" (new converts) at the bottom and ensured that Berg's extended "Royal Family" remained in total control. As an autocratic messiah, he claimed to have direct communication with God—the Lord's "Moses" for today. His word was unquestioned, and even "murmuring" against his views was considered a mortal sin. Parents were to be hated and despised along with the corrupt political system of the United States. In fact, he prophesied America's destruction when the comet Kahoutek would collide with Earth.

Berg and most of his disciples left behind their doomed native land and set up operations in Europe. His whereabouts remains unknown, though COG international headquarters are in Zurich, and it is rumored that Berg has gone into secluded hiding somewhere in Switzerland.

The practices of COG stir volatile reactions wherever they go. Though Berg once applied for Israeli citizenship, he eventually turned violently anti-Semitic. He courted the favor of Libya's Qaddafi and said about Jews, "devils incarnate . . . if I had a gun I'd shoot them myself!"

Commune members languish in often unsanitary quarters, are sometimes refused medical treatment, and are kept on a subsistence diet of food "procured" from local

Symbol
None known except the ubiquitous folded MO letters handed out to passing motorists or pedestrians.

supermarkets. The "Revolutionary Contract" they sign turns over all possessions to the COG, and most contacts with past friends and family are abruptly severed, unless such individuals are considered sources of revenue for the group. Negative comments are forbidden, no member is ever left alone, and daily hours that are not spent pouring over MO letters are dedicated to "litnessing"—evangelizing by literature distribution. Litnessing is also a primary source of cult income with strict quotas set as a barometer of fervency for the cause.

SEXUAL THEOLOGY

Another basic source of income is through what amounts to religious prostitution, called "FFing" ("flirty fishing") in COG parlance. Female members are encouraged to offer their bodies as an inducement for men to join the organization, though the "fish" are expected to pay for such favors. Husbands are admonished to offer their wives as a symbol of their devotion to the cause. If venereal disease is contracted (Berg admits he himself is afflicted), it is seen as a willingness to suffer for the cause of Christ. In fact, Berg asserts that Jesus practiced sexual intercourse with Mary and Martha and deliberately contracted venereal disease to illustrate his identification with human infirmities.

Sex is a central theme of the salacious MO letters. Nothing is forbidden. Even homosexuality and oral sodomy, which were once considered taboo, have now been legitimized "within the limits of the love of God." Childhood sex is advocated, and children conceived through FFing are called "Jesus Babes." (Unwed mothers are euphemistically referred to as "widows.") Topless bathing is promoted; girls are admonished not to wear undergarments.

A marriage relationship (approved of first by colony leaders) consists of simply going to bed with the chosen partner—legal civil ceremonies are seen as part of Babylon's corrupt system. Lesbianism and incest are considered particularly desirable.

Berg's system of sexual philosophy also includes the following: wife-swapping—justified by the "all things in common" passage of Acts 2:44; punishing female members by requiring them to masturbate before male observers; fondling children and sleeping with them in the nude; and the belief that God had intercourse with Mary to procreate Jesus! "God is in the business of breaking up families . . . salvation sets us free from the curse of clothing and the shame of nakedness," Berg writes. "God is a pimp," he blasphemously declares, ". . . ex-

---

Address/Location
World publication headquarters in Zurich, Switzerland. Colony addresses available for most major U.S. cities.

perience a spiritual orgasm by being filled with the Spirit."

When questioned about his personal sexual excesses, Berg argues that he is God's King David, and that like his namesake, his own sexual promiscuity has been condoned by the Almighty.

The most startling aspect of Berg's sexual obsessions is his claim to indulge in succubus relationships—sexual intercourse with spirit beings whom he calls "goddesses." In fact, Berg has a long history of flirtation with the occult. He contends that "spiritual counselors" visit him regularly and even enter his body to speak through his mouth. One of them, Abrahim, is supposedly a gypsy king who has been dead for over 1,000 years. Berg has also been involved in palmistry, fortune-telling, and astrology. "Spiritualistic churches are not so bad after all," he concludes.

DEFECTORS ABOUND
In Berg's eyes, the COG are the 144,000 of Revelation 7 and 14, the restored Israel. After the United States falls to communism, the anti-Christ will briefly reign until Satan takes over. The majority of professing Christians will take the mark of the beast, but the COG will remain the Lord's faithful. In spite of his unimpressive record of past prophecies, the end, according to Berg, will come in 1993. Non-COG members need not fear, however, since Berg's universalist theology

leaves room for a second chance; few will be left to inhabit hell. In fact, those living can even now pray people out of hell.

Berg's coarse language (MO letters are spiced with four-letter expletives) and immoral philosophy may have finally taken its toll. Defectors abound, including his Barbara Cane ("Queen Rachel") who was Berg's heir apparent. Even the most effectively brainwashed followers of cult leaders cannot per-

Deviations
At times Berg denies the Trinity ("I don't believe in the Trinity"). On other occasions he has promoted a Father, Mother, and Son conglomerate. The Holy Spirit, "Holy Queen of Love," is portrayed as a half-naked woman. Christ is declared to be a created being in a misinterpretation of Revelation 3:14. Scriptural injunctions against consulting familiar spirits are ignored (Deut. 18:9-14; Jer. 14:14) by communicating with what Berg calls "God's Witches." Berg also denies God's promises of blessings to the Jews (Acts 3:18-26; Rom. 9:4, 5) by cursing "May God damn the God-damned Jews." By encouraging fornication, polygamy, incest, and adultery, Berg stands in opposition to the biblical view of sex in marriage as expressed in Hebrews 13 and Ephesians 5. In his rebellion against the historic church, Berg has, in the words of anticult researcher Jack Sparks, "managed to transform a gigantic personal temper tantrum against authority into a worldwide movement."

manently overlook their leader's delusions of grandeur and his claims of divine endorsement. As Carole Hausmann and Gretchen Passantino put it in *The New Cults,* "The Holy Spirit is not some love potion. The Father is not some oversexed god. The Son is not a promiscuous bachelor with V.D." That conclusion has also apparently been reached by more than one former COG member.

UPDATE

Officials in Britain requested a report concerning the handing out of leaflets by COG members who were soliciting shoppers for money. It was reported that the leaflet told of COG girls working in "escort" agencies in London, gave advice, interspersed with an occasional "TYJ" (Thank You, Jesus), and amounted practically to instruction in prostitution.

Hundreds of members of the COG are living a vagabond existence in small groups throughout the Federal Republic of Germany, according to a December 1984, report by the parents' association A.G.P.F. It was also reported that COG founder David "Moses" Berg, who had been given shelter by Libyan leader Qaddafi, has organized an international call-girl ring.

In 1984, Berg's daughter Deborah (Linda Berg) Davis published a book detailing her father's secretive cult practices. Deborah, who now professes to be an orthodox evangelical Christian, says the movement was corrupt from the beginning and she herself was nearly driven to commit suicide.

Seven Ways to Relate to a Cult Member

It's one thing to know what a cult is and what it believes. It's another to know how to relate to cult members personally, face to face, and how to deal with them when you encounter them in public places or even in more personal, social situations.

Here are some ideas to help you relate warmly and effectively to cult members.

1. Don't hesitate to say no. You don't want to support the cult, so don't buy anything (flowers, candles, books, gifts). You can offer a polite refusal and still engage that person in conversation.

2. Don't hesitate to say, "I don't know." Admit it. You don't know all the answers. You're not an expert in apologetics, comparative religions, or theology. If you don't know an answer, say so, then point the cult member to another source where the answer may be found.

3. Don't assume that they "know all the answers." Many times cult members seem confident and assured in their beliefs, but deep down they have questions and doubts that trouble them. Appeal to this insecurity; try to steer the conversation beyond theological issues and points of debate toward matters of the heart and spirit.

4. *Express your humanness—that you are sinful and need salvation.* Many cults demand perfection from their members, and it becomes refreshing to some of them to meet one who is less than perfect, yet still secure in his or her faith. Don't let your faith become phony, a front, or an act. Don't try to be something you aren't.

5. *Be hopeful and cheerful.* You'd be surprised how far a smile will go with someone who is searching for God.

6. *Try to be on the offensive, not the defensive.* You shouldn't have to prove yourself to them; they're the ones trying to sell you something, remember? Don't let them intimidate you by the attitude that they're "more spiritual than you are."

7. *Buy the person a cup of coffee.* By this action you are saying, "I care about you even though I don't agree with you." Remember that members of most cults are lured by the feelings of love and warmth generated by the cult group; they need to see that people outside of the cult can be just as caring.

Cults and Christianity Compared

GOD

Christian Theology. Both the Old and New Testament proclaim the triune nature of God—Father, Son, and Holy Spirit. They are co-equal, co-existent, and co-eternal, three Persons of the same Substance (John 1:1-3; 14:26). God is a personality who can speak and create and who possesses a mind and will (Gen. 1:1, 26; Jer. 29:11; Ezek. 18:30). God's character is eternal (1 Tim. 1:17), omnipotent (Rev. 19:6), omnipresent (Ps. 139:7-12), omniscient (Rom. 11:33), perfect (Deut. 32:4), and holy (1 Pet. 1:16).

Supporting Scriptures
1. 1 Cor. 8:6—". . . there is but one God, the Father, of whom are all things. . . ."
2. Isa. 43:10—". . . before me there was no God formed, neither shall there be after me."
3. Exod. 3:14—"And God said unto Moses, I AM THAT I AM. . . ."
4. 1 Tim. 2:5—"For there is one God. . . ."

5. Ps. 90:2—". . . from everlasting to everlasting, thou art God."

Cult Doctrine
1. Impersonal, unknowable essence (Hinduism, Bahaism).
2. Divine idea, principle, or example (Christian Science, Unity).
3. Non-trinitarianism (Jehovah's Witnesses, The Way).

CHRIST

Christian Theology. The Apostles' Creed states: "Conceived by the Holy Ghost, born of the Virgin Mary, suffered under Pontius Pilate, died and was buried; He descended into Hell; the third day He arose from the dead; He ascended into Heaven and sitteth on the right hand of God the Father Almighty; from thence He shall come to judge the quick and the dead." Jesus Christ is the second Person of the Trinity, the eternally Begotten Son of God who became flesh and is now our "great high priest, that is passed into the heavens . . . [who] was in all points tempted like as we are, yet without sin" (Heb. 4:14, 15).

Supporting Scriptures
1. John 1:1, 3—"In the beginning was the Word, and the Word was with God, and the Word was God. . . . All things were made by him; and without him was not any thing made. . . ."

2. John 1:14—"And the Word was made flesh and dwelt among us, (and we beheld his glory, the glory as of the only begotten of the Father). . . ."
3. 1 John 4:3—". . . every spirit that confesseth not that Jesus Christ is come in the flesh is not of God; and this is the spirit of antichrist. . . ."
4. Eph. 1:21—"Far above all principality, and power, and might, and dominion, and every name that is named. . . ."
5. Col. 2:9—"For in him dwelleth all the fulness of the Godhead bodily. . . ."

Cult Doctrine
1. Merely a human being without divinity who attained "Christ Consciousness" (The Church Universal and Triumphant, The International Community of Christ).
2. Created being (Mormonism, Jehovah's Witnesses).
3. One of many *avatars* or revelations of God (Hinduism, Divine Light Mission).

MAN
Christian Theology. God created man in his own image (Gen. 1:26), perfect and without sin so that he could know and love God. Man is the highest distinction of God's creative genius, separate from him, made "a little lower than the angels" (Ps. 8:5) with dominion over all the earth (Gen. 1:28). In Eden, man fell by disobedience; henceforth all men are conceived in sin with a depraved nature

destined for damnation unless they are spiritually reborn (John 3:3).

Supporting Scriptures
1. Jer. 17:9—"The heart is deceitful above all things, and desperately wicked. . . ."
2. Rom. 5:12—". . . by one man sin entered into the world, and death by sin; . . . all have sinned."
3. Rom. 5:19—"For as by one man's disobedience many were made sinners. . . ."
4. Ps. 51:5—". . . in sin did my mother conceive me."
5. Rom. 1:21—". . . their foolish heart was darkened."

Cult Doctrine
1. Divine, an emanation of the infinite Impersonal (Theosophy, Rosicrucianism).
2. Sinful but capable of attaining the same "Christ Consciousness" that Jesus did (Church Universal and Triumphant, Holy Order of MANS).
3. Destined to be a god (Mormonism, Worldwide Church of God).

ATONEMENT
Christian Theology. The Old Testament sacrifices foreshadowed the Lamb of God, "slain from the foundation of the world" (Rev. 13:8), whose shed blood would be the final sacrifice and cleansing for sin (1 John 1:7). Man, whose sinful rebellion has separated him from God, can now have "peace through

the blood of his cross" (Col. 1:20) and be "reconciled" to God (2 Cor. 5:19) because of his vicarious, substitutionary death.

Supporting Scriptures
1. 1 Pet. 2:24—"Who his own self bare our sins in his own body on the tree. . . ."
2. Rom. 5:8—". . . while we were yet sinners, Christ died for us."
3. Acts 4:12—"Neither is there salvation in any other: for there is none other name under heaven given among men, whereby we must be saved."
4. Heb. 9:22—". . . without shedding of blood is no remission."
5. 1 John 1:9—"If we confess our sins, he is faithful and just to forgive us our sins, and to cleanse us from all unrighteousness."

Cult Doctrine
1. Good works and beneficent deeds will cause one to achieve at-one-ment with God (Unity, Bahaism).
2. Reincarnation will fulfill the law of karma (Scientology, Krishna Consciousness).
3. Universalism; all will eventually be saved (Mormonism, Christian Science).

REVELATION
Christian Theology. The Word of God in scriptural canon is inspired (God-breathed), inerrant, complete (Rev. 22:18, 19), and the only infallible rule of faith. It reveals the origin and destiny of all things; records God's dealings with mankind in the past, present,

and future; and focuses on the Person and work of Jesus Christ. The Bible inspires faith (Rom. 10:17) and will make men "wise unto salvation" (2 Tim. 3:15).

Supporting Scriptures
1. 2 Tim. 3:16—"All scripture is given by inspiration of God, and is profitable for doctrine, for reproof, for correction, for instruction in righteousness."
2. 2 Pet. 1:21—". . . holy men of God spake as they were moved by the Holy Ghost."
3. Ps. 119:105—"Thy word is a lamp unto my feet, and a light unto my path."
4. Isa. 40:8—". . . the word of our God shall stand for ever."
5. Heb. 4:12—"For the word of God is quick, and powerful, and sharper than any two-edged sword . . . and is a discerner of the thoughts and intents of the heart."

Cult Doctrine
1. The Bible needs additional subjective or written revelation for our age (Mormonism, The Walk).
2. The Word of God needs to be properly translated with accompanying explanations (Jehovah's Witnesses, The Way).
3. The Bible is one of many equally divine, sacred books (Unity, Bahaism).

Cult Information Resources

Several evangelical organizations are dedicated to keeping watch on cult activities. These parachurch service agencies are generally very cooperative when requested to supply information regarding both newly formed and already established cults.

Bob Larson Ministries
P.O. Box 36480
Denver, CO 80236

Christian Apologetics Project
P.O. Box 105
Absecon, NJ 08201

Christian Apologetics:
Research & Information Service (CARIS)
P.O. Box 2067
Costa Mesa, CA 92626

Christian Ministry to Cults
P.O. Box M-507
Hoboken, NJ 07030

Christian Research Institute
P.O. Box 500
San Juan Capistrano, CA 97693

Institute of Contemporary Christianity
P.O. Box A
Oakland, NJ 07436

*Spiritual Counterfeits Project
P.O. Box 2418
Berkeley, CA 94702

*Additional listings of other agencies offering anticult information are available here. It is the author's opinion that this organization is the most scholarly and comprehensive source of cult information available.

Coercive Cult Techniques

Loneliness, indecision, despair, and disappointment are the emotional characteristics cult recruiters notice. They approach the unwary with an excessively friendly invitation to a lecture, free meal, weekend workshop, or other activity offering instant solutions to overwhelming problems. Surprisingly enough, few potential cultists bother to inquire about who is extending the offer, what is behind it, and what functions will take place. Vague answers are seldom challenged, leaving the recruiter an unassailable opportunity to obscure his intentions.

Even given the current anticult climate, few targets of the cults see their future as one of involuntary slavery and physical domination. Before joining any exotic sect, one should be aware of what could result: neurosis, psychosis, suicidal tendencies, guilt, identity confusion, paranoia, hallucinations, loss of free will, intellectual sterility, and diminished capacity of judgment. It will be much easier to avoid such consequences by identifying and recognizing the following psychological forms of "cult-coercion."

1. *Absolute loyalty.* Allegiance to the sect is demanded and enforced by actual or veiled threats to one's body or eternal spiritual condition.
2. *Altered diet.* Depriving one of essential nutrients and enforcing a low-protein diet can lead to disorientation and emotional susceptibility.
3. *Chanting and meditation.* Objective intellectual input is avoided by countering anticult questions with repetitious songs and chants.
4. *Conformity.* Dress, language, names, and interests take on a sameness which erodes individuality.
5. *Doctrinal confusion.* Incomprehensible "truths" are more readily accepted when presented in a complex fashion which encourages rejection of logical thought.
6. *Exclusivity.* Those outside the cult are viewed as spiritually inferior, creating an exclusive attitude of the self-righteous "we" versus "they" mentality.
7. *Financial involvement.* All or part of one's personal assets may be donated to the cult, increasing a vested interest in sticking-with-it and lessening the chance of returning to a former vocation.
8. *Hypnotic states.* Inducing a highly susceptible state of mind may be accom-

plished by chanting, repetitious singing, or meditation.

9. *Isolation from outside.* Diminished perception of reality results when one is physically separated from friends, society, and the rational frame of reference in which one has previously functioned.

10. *Lack of privacy.* Reflective, critical thinking is impossible in a setting where cult members are seldom left unattended.

11. *Love-bombing.* Physical affection and constant contrived attention can give a false sense of camaraderie.

12. *Megacommunication.* Long, confusing lectures can be an effective tool if the inductee is bombarded with glib rhetoric and catch phrases.

13. *New relationships.* Marriage to another cult member and the destruction of past family relationships integrates one fully into the cult "family."

14. *Nonsensical activities.* Games and other activities with no apparent purpose leave one dependent upon a group or leader to give direction and order.

15. *Pavlovian control.* Behavior modification by alternating reward and punishment leads to confusion and dependency.

16. *Peer pressure.* By exploiting one's desire for acceptance, doubts about cult practices can be overcome by offering a sense of belonging to an affirming community.

17. *Sensory deprivation.* Fatigue coupled with prolonged activity can make one vulnerable to otherwise offensive beliefs and suggestions.
18. *Surrendered privacy.* The ego's normal emotional defensive mechanisms can easily be stripped away by having the new member share personal secrets which can later be used for intimidation.
19. *Unquestioning submission.* Acceptance of cult practices is achieved by discouraging any questions or natural curiosity which may challenge what the leaders propagate.
20. *Value rejection.* As the recruit becomes more integrated into the cult, he is encouraged to denounce the values and beliefs of his former life.

Recommended Reading

The books listed below represent sources of information concerning cults for the reader who wishes to investigate more thoroughly a particular group or teaching.

1. Robert and Gretchen Passantino, *Answers to the Cultist at Your Door,* Harvest House Publishers, Eugene, OR, 1981.
2. Gordon R. Lewis, *Confronting the Cults,* The Presbyterian and Reformed Publishing Co., Oklahoma City, OK, 1966.
3. Edmond C. Gruss, *Cults and the Occult,* Baker Book House, Grand Rapids, MI, 1974.
4. Kenneth Boa, *Cults, World Religions and You,* Victor Books, Wheaton, IL, 1977.
5. John H. Garabedian and Orde Coombs, *Eastern Religions in the Electric Age,* Grosset and Dunlap, Workman Publishing Co., New York, NY, 1969.

6. J. Gordon Melton, *(The) Encyclopedia of American Religions, Vols. 1 and 2,* McGrath Publishing Co., Wilmington, NC, 1978.

7. National Geographic Society, *Great Religions of the World,* 1971.

8. Robert Morey, *How to Answer a Jehovah's Witness,* Bethany Fellowship, Inc., Minneapolis, MN, 1980.

9. Walter Martin, *(The) Kingdom of the Cults,* Bethany Fellowship, Inc., Minneapolis, MN, 1977.

10. David Breese, *Know the Mark of the Cults,* Victor Books, Wheaton, IL, 1980.

11. Ronald Enroth, *(The) Lure of the Cults,* Christian Herald Books, Chappaqua, NY, 1979.

12. Jack Sparks, *(The) Mind Benders,* Thomas Nelson, Inc., Publishers, Nashville, TN, 1977.

13. Pat Means, *(The) Mystical Maze,* Campus Crusade for Christ, Inc., San Bernardino, CA, 1976 (out of print).

14. Walter Martin, *(The) New Cults,* Vision House, Santa Ana, CA, 1980.

15. John Weldon and Clifford Wilson, *Occult Shock and Psychic Forces,* Master Books, San Diego, CA, 1980.

16. James and Marcia Rudin, *Prison or Paradise?,* Fortress Press, Philadelphia, PA, 1980.

17. Robert A. Morey, *Reincarnation and Christianity,* Bethany Fellowship, Inc., Minneapolis, MN, 1980.

18. Gerald L. Berry, *Religions of the World,*

Barnes and Noble, Harper and Row, New York, NY, 1965.

19. Walter Martin, *Rise of the Cults,* Vision House, Santa Ana, CA, 1980.

20. Flo Conway and Jim Siegelman, *Snapping,* J. B. Lippincott Co., Philadelphia, PA, 1978.

21. William J. Petersen, *Those Curious New Cults,* Keats Publishing Co., New Canaan, CT, 1975.

22. J. L. Williams, *Victor Paul Wierwille and The Way International,* Moody Press, Chicago, IL, 1979.

23. Ronald Enroth, *Youth, Brainwashing, and the Extremist Cults,* Zondervan Publishing House, Grand Rapids, MI, 1977.

About the Author

BOB LARSON is president of Bob Larson Ministries in Denver, Colorado. He has lectured in more than seventy countries on the subject of contemporary culture and is the author of *Larson's Book of Cults* and *Rock,* both published by Tyndale House. He currently hosts a daily television talk show, Talk-Back with Bob Larson.

POCKET GUIDES
NEW FROM TYNDALE

■ *Getting Out of Debt* by Howard L. Dayton, Jr. At last, a no-nonsense approach to your money problems. Here's advice on creating a budget, cutting corners, making investments, and paying off loans. Features a list of money-saving tips.

■ *Hi-Fidelity Marriage* by J. Allen Petersen. A respected family counselor shows you how to start an affair—with your own spouse. Learn how to keep love alive . . . rekindle old flames . . . grow from mistakes. You have what it takes to make your marriage better.

■ *Increase Your Personality Power* by Tim La-Haye. Why do you get angry? Afraid? Worried? Discover your unique personality type, then use it to live more effectively—at home, on the job, and under pressure. An easy-to-use format includes personality tests to take on your own.

■ *The Perfect Way to Lose Weight* by Charles T. Kuntzleman and Daniel V. Runyon. Anyone can lose fat—and keep it off permanently. This tested program, developed by a leading physical fitness expert, shows how. Helpful charts and safety tips round out this practical fat-loss plan.

■ *Temper Your Child's Tantrums* by Dr. James Dobson. You don't need to feel frustrated as a parent. The celebrated author and "Focus on the Family" radio host wants to give you the keys to firm, but loving, discipline in your home. Follow his proven counsel and watch the difference in your children.